ONLY

THE

WORLD

ONLY
THE
WORLD

Constance Urdang

UNIVERSITY OF PITTSBURGH PRESS

8/1983
am. Lit.

Published by the University of Pittsburgh Press, Pittsburgh, Pa. 15260
Copyright © 1983, Constance Urdang
Feffer and Simons, Inc., London
Manufactured in the United States of America

Library of Congress Cataloging in Publication Data

Urdang, Constance.
  Only the world.

  (Pitt poetry series)
  I. Title. II. Series.
PS3571.R305   1983   811'.54   82-20062
ISBN 0-8229-3477-9
ISBN 0-8229-5349-8 (pbk.)

Acknowledgment is made to the following publications for permission to re-print some of the poems that appear in this book: *New England Review, Perspective, Ploughshares, Poetry Now,* and *Yankee.*

"Another Traveler" and "Traveling Light" are reprinted by permission from *National Forum: The Phi Kappa Phi Journal,* Vol. LXI, No. 3, p. 12; "The Cold Country" appeared in Vol. LXII, No. 1, p. 31. "Clouds," "Night Air," and "The Other Life" originally appeared in *Poetry.* "Why They Turned Back/Why They Went On" first appeared in *The Chariton Review* (Fall 1981).

*The publication of this book is supported by grants
from the National Endowment for the Arts
in Washington, D.C., a Federal agency,
and the Pennsylvania Council on the Arts.*

There is no world of appearances, there is only the world.

—*Martin Buber,* I and Thou

CONTENTS

CONTENTS

III

I

TRAVELING LIGHT

Reading that Florence Johnson and Reva Barron
Are about to set out for the silk-trade routes of China
Via Little Tibet in the Himalayas,
"Almost as isolated as Tibet itself,"
Taking in Nepal, Burma, and Thailand
As well as "the site of the greatest
Archaeological discovery of recent times,"
I see them in the light
Shed by a dauntless queue of female travelers
Breaking out of the cage of civilization,
Some in long skirts and pith helmets, armed with umbrellas,
Who followed the moon to Morocco, braved
The harsh and splendid Souff, traversed
All Asia on wild, incomprehensible journeys,
Or marched in an alien sunlight
Toward the shifting horizons of Connecticut,
That gentle landscape barren of mystery,
No wolves in the thin plantations of lilac and birch,
Yet where they might also remark, "I see no wonder
In this shrubbery, equal to seeing myself in it."

BRAZIL

Preferring travel books to travel
There will always be those who
Will never visit Brazil
Or set off with four natives in a canoe
In pouring rain, paddling up savage rivers;
Only in dreams
They touch down amid exuberant foliage
Sinking into the embrace
Of those moist, ardent airs,
Tuning their ears
To skin-drum and nose-flute,
Scenting at a distance
"The authentic smell of danger."

Blazing no trail, claiming no territory,
Confronting the sublimities of nature
On toothy peaks and boiling seas
"Singularly unmoved," at ease
Among companions forever congenial,
For them all else can be dispensed with
But history taken from Shakespeare,
Geography from Robinson Crusoe,
And the mangroves and swamps of Brazil
Where they will never set foot.

THE LUGGAGE

Travel is a vanishing act
Only to those who are left behind.
What the traveler knows
Is that he accompanies himself,
Unwieldy baggage that can't be checked,
Stolen, or lost, or mistaken.
So one took, past outposts of empire,
"Calmly as if in the British Museum,"
Not only her Victorian skirts,
Starched shirtwaists, and umbrella, but her faith
In the civilizing mission of women,
Her backaches and insomnia, her innocent valor;
Another, friend of witch-doctors,
Living on native chop,
Trading tobacco and hooks for fish and fetishes,
Heralded her astonishing arrival
Under shivering stars
By calling, "It's only me!" A third,
Intent on savage customs, and to demonstrate
That a woman could travel as easily as a man,
Carried a handkerchief damp with wifely tears
And only once permitted a tribal chieftain
To stroke her long, golden hair.

THE WISH TO LEAVE HOME

I don't go there any more,
To that imaginary place called home
Where past my tall pale window a red sun
Perpetually shrinks behind the Palisades;
But I imagine I can see a girl,
Adrift in the terrible ennui of adolescence,
Her elbows on the sill, leaning into the dreaming air.
The journeying mood is on her, she thinks of nothing
But getting away. She knows a ship is waiting
Somewhere in the harbor, with all sails set, but she
Is still imprisoned in the tower
That leans into the sunset above the river.

THE TWO LADIES

Wherever you travel, there are two English ladies
Who share the expenses of a little house,
Drink gin or milky tea together, and know all
About where to find whatever you're looking for.
Weather permitting, one is bulky in tweeds,
The other, in boyish gabardine, is trim.
Life is not always easy, amid the lush flowering
Of alien customs and currencies, foreign dishes,
Dank shops where the most commonplace groceries
Can't be obtained, and nobody speaks English;
But they make a virtue of inconvenience,
In "the happy lands where it is always afternoon."
Like the Ladies of Llangollen, "the 2 most celebrated
Virgins in Europe," who themselves became an attraction
For the better class of tourists, they ask only
To live as they please, under a kindly sun.

ANOTHER TRAVELER

Carrying before her
Her face of a German *Fraülein*
Wholesome as fresh milk,
Bold as Leatherstocking
She marched over the curdled ocean
Toward Niagaras of savages;
It is one of those incomprehensible journeys,
Leaving behind everything that is known
For the sake of *Ultima Thule*.

At thirty years of age
Come to a jumping-off place,
The landscape flattened to a shrubbery
Devoid of wonders,
She sees a white road
Winding toward shifting horizons,
Her new found land,
Its vistas unexplored,
Her destiny in a teacup.

THE ALIEN

Was it chance that brought him here
Over an ocean wider and deeper
Than he could ever have imagined
To the dream-country of torrential Niagaras,
Of forests impenetrable, rivers and lakes like oceans,
A continent split by canyons grand enough
To have swallowed whole the boulevards,
The soft stones, of Vienna and Munich,
Berlin's old linden trees, bowed under history?
Surely it must have seemed easier,
So cosy, guttural, and *gemütlich,*
To stay home with the others. Perhaps
It was more than chance that drove him, for
A lifetime later, guileless as the youth
Who stepped ashore in 1929
Out of the Black Forest into a black year,
He is still wondering at the blackness in
Men's hearts, that is not bounded
By oceans or geography.

WHY THEY TURNED BACK/
WHY THEY WENT ON

Because a black bird flew across the road;
Because the attendant at the pump turned surly;
Because the uncertain weather
Made Mother nervous,
And, back home, the telephone kept ringing
In an empty house;
Because a white bird flew across the road.

How far had they come?
How far did they go?

Seeing, along river after river,
Between shores of brush and willow,
Only the bend ahead and the bend behind
Under a sky featureless and hard
As a shallow bowl; through tautologies
Of a landscape unendingly repeated
Mile after mile; down Main Street
After Main Street, replications
Of the same petty civic scenery;
Hearing the ghosts of trains
Crossing between cornfields,
Clattering over the points, moaning
Above creosote and cinders,
As if the imagination
Could produce nothing more
Than the same landscape, cornfields,
Rivers, and Main Streets
Pulling them, like a magnet, not *toward*
But *away from*, not into the future,
But away from the past;

Until a white bird flew across the road
With its mysterious message, that said to some,
"Turn back," and to the rest, "Go on."

ELENA

I don't know Chicago, but somewhere
On its grid of avenues
Elena walks, her honey-slow smile
Frozen by the gales
Under the El, learning to live
On Rush Street, in the accelerated tempo
Of the Promised Land, learning
The lessons of Poverty, the lessons of
Unskilled, the lessons of Hispanic.
Do the weeds of Second-Class-Citizen suit her?
Two thousand miles from Chicago, in a kinder air,
She might blossom again like the bougainvillaea,
Her sweetness cascading
Over the crumbling walls in torrents
Of purple and red, those royal colors. Instead,
Lured northward in pursuit of gold
As once the Spaniards sailed the southern seas
In search of Montezuma's treasure,
She paces the bitter boulevards of Chicago.

COLD COUNTRY

The cold country dreams of fires
On glowing hearths cosy as Christmas,
Of ovens and stoves, steam
Rising from peppery stews.
The cold country imagines itself
As a single snow-covered hillside,
Rural, remote, and silent,
Inhabited only by a stand of pines.
The cold country wraps itself in quilts;
In thick socks and mittens it sallies forth
Imagining tropics of infinite *calor,*
Days drenched in stifling sunshine,
Gaudy flame-colored sunsets,
And hot nights of blue velvet
Pierced with stars like burning rivets.

The cold county shivers
In a bleak street of ancient tenements
Where men in woolen hats and galoshes, women
Bundled in shapeless coats, are picking their way
Across partially frozen slush.
Here the cold country is at home
Beneath a filigree of old-fashioned fire-escapes.
It is the capital of the cold country,
Where the laws are made
And sentences carried out.
In cramped apartments on a cheerless staircase
The cold country settles down.

THE STEEP STREETS

Longing to lose himself
In the steep, stony streets
Where all through the morning
Roosters crow in peremptory voices, shrill
With the cadence of hopefulness;
Where the rain, when it comes,
Comes suddenly and hard,
Weeping all night in the flowering trees,
He keeps going back,
Stumbling toward his separate destiny
As Karl Wallenda, that obstinate old man,
Walked to his on the wire.

It's treacherous underfoot
On the greasy, sharp cobbles
Older than Columbus;
When night presses down,
Exhaling its breath of lilies,
A single light bulb burns in the little shop
Where daytimes the old woman sells
Coffee, soap powder, bread,
And one or two eggs.
He'll always be alien here. What draws him back,
Lugging his heavy baggage? What sirens call him,
A tightrope walker, to his windy fate?

IN THE GARDEN

If I were to take root here
It would be as that nameless tree,
The one with a hundred hungry gray snouts
Nuzzling into the ferns, or that other one
With foliage of brilliant feathers.
Part of me would flourish
In the shadow of an ancient rock,
Its vegetable surfaces so dark,
Secret, and moist, new life-forms spring there,
Incomprehensible words become green flesh;
Or, in the shadeless noon,
I'd sprout impossible blossoms
Heavy with sunlight and the weight
Of a regiment of drunken bees.
With a thousand green fingers
I'd cling to that wall,
The little airs of the garden
Humming in all my throats.

DRIVING INTO THE OZARKS

Driving down into the Ozarks
The dusty roads edged with mullein
And Queen Anne's lace
Unroll like filmstrips, or memories of home,
And a thousand miles inland
A child puts a shell to his ear
Because the history of the ocean
Is recorded in echoes,
And because all the while
The little waves are nibbling at the coastline
So that one day
America will begin at the Ozarks.

COMING HOME

Alighting in a climate grown unfamiliar
And harsher than he remembered
To find the station platform deserted
No old friends waiting impatiently in borrowed cars
To clasp him in warm arms, and the train that delivered him
Already shrinking in the distance; or thumbing through
The telephone directory with blind fingers
To find the numbers have all been changed
Is only another way of discovering
That he is what has altered; citizens here
Have continued to go about their business.
Throughout the uncounted years of his fitful
Odyssey-faring, they have been riding to work
Past the same subway stops, seldom complaining;
A little more grizzled, perhaps, heavier,
Returning at nightfall to the same cramped apartments
He remembers with nostalgia, as if they were history.
If something is missing, a space, or a vacant chair
In the picture, only he is aware
Of the empty place, and what might have belonged there.

WAYS OF RETURNING

Returning through the back streets, through alleys so narrow
The walls of the houses part like grass
Leaning backward, their patience demonstrated
By scarred plaster, worm-eaten sills, and,
Thrust through a chalk-blue door,
A clenched brass fist, everything the same
As it was, the sun, boys shooting marbles the same,
The same flies buzzing minarets of garbage, the same fists;
Or skating across the enormous mirrored spaces
Of an airport, in St. Louis or anywhere,
Passing the snack bars, the budget rent-a-car, electronic games,
Seeing the men and women queued up to telephone
To say to someone, to anyone
At the end of the line, Hello, it's me,
I'm back; or, after driving all day long
To come into town at nightfall, the avenues
Festooned with lights, every block so familiar
You catch a glimpse of yourself coming down the street,
Yourself, in a coat you wore then, carrying something
You carried then, or maybe are carrying still.

AESTHETICS OF ESCAPE

This is the country everyone wants to escape to,
These mild hills speckled with sunlight, this tawny plain;
Down the long corridor between the mountains
A soft wind moans. The people pray for rain.
Driving the difficult road this afternoon
Rutted, and pitted with pot-holes, steep, twisting along
The mountain's unguarded ridges, weaving between
Dangerous trucks that belch fire and smoke like dragons
And buses that might be comic, such rattles and groans
Are wrung from them as they bustle over the stones,
The landscape unrolls alongside like a tapestry.
The skittering goats are aesthetic, and the ragged children
Embroider the scene. At nightfall in the square
How picturesque are the people in their pageantry,
How serious the look on the face of the saint
Who is carried shoulder-high down the dusty street
So the rain will come and the children need not go hungry.
But that is no waxen babe in the tiny coffin,
Dressed like an angel, and wreathed around with flowers.
In the cavern of the church the candles flicker
Making the shadows dance. This is the country
Of everyone's dreams, from which there is no escaping.

THE WISH TO SETTLE DOWN

And some journey not as pilgrims, but are carried along
On an endless conveyor belt, crisscrossing their lives
Without a stopping-place, like the *Flying Dutchman*
Traversing the ocean of sky, or the Wandering Jew
Forever on the move, their destiny
A series of provincial capitals;
In one they think maybe they'll settle down,
Buy a geranium for the window sill,
Join AA, study French, lose weight,
Compare notes on the weather with the neighbors;
But something intervenes, it won't work out.
Weary of moving, once more they move on
To try a foreign city or a farm,
Their only resting place the final one.

II

THE WILL TO BELIEVE

Look at your palm, the lines
Etched deep as the day you were born;
They must mean something.
Or handwriting; if you could read it,
How it reveals all you thought
You could hide, how gaudy, boisterous,
And flamboyant you are inside;
Invisible hands bend spoons, or do I do it
From another room? If I were the gypsy
In pungent red satin, I'd see the tall dark man,
Good fortune coming, maybe tomorrow, in tea leaves;
And the old *abuelita*, to her the veritable Face
Of the Virgin will appear on a tortilla, and they'll frame it
Under glass, and the miracle will be
Two thousand pilgrims in pickups and old sedans
Driving a thousand miles across the desert to see it.

MINIMALISTS

*In the old days they ate buffalo; now
they eat radishes.*

These days take the wish for the deed, as certain painters,
Disdaining brush and palette, dictate a landscape
In one or two shorthand sentences, or describe
A masterpiece, ideal because unrealized on canvas,
In lieu of what was called art. The mundane part,
The skill, the doing, the craft, is scorned
In times like ours, so why not eliminate
What really happened, and replace it with
What one might have preferred, the daring deeds
Undone, races unwon, adventures not attempted?
Not a new trick; Vespucci, even,
They say, left two sets of letters, "both purporting
To describe his expeditions, but full
Of inexplicable contradictions," until
There is no way of knowing which is history,
Or if he ever touched the fabulous shores
Named for him, the Americas; and Frederick Cook
Laid claim to the North Pole, but none was there
To see him—and what charms us, is the doubt.
There's a perverseness in our times, that relishes
These tantalizing ambivalences, delighting
In the question more than the answer, the telling
More than the truth. It maddened Crowhurst,
Who knew himself unfit to be a hero
But schemed to seem one, calculating how
To show by logbooks he had sailed nonstop
Around the world, to win the glorious race;
Instead, the perfect hero for our time,
Minimalist of adventure, he left only
An empty craft with but one mizzen sail
Ghosting along in the Sargasso Sea.

ONLY THE WORLD

The two tall cypresses and their three lean sisters
Farther down the hill, bowing and swaying,
Formal as nuns in their dark habits, silent
Under the wind, patient in the dry season,
Must they stand for something?
And the vermilion bird, like a tongue of flame,
And the bird called jump-over-the-wall, and the nameless one
Who learns a new tune every morning, must they also
Signify? The sharp, uneven cobbles
And the dust that seeps in everywhere
And the children's plaintive cries
That are carried away on the wind:
They are only the world.
It is enough.

CLOUDS

You might say that clouds have no nationality
Being flags of no country, flaunting their innocent neutrality
Across frontiers, ignorant of boundaries;
But these clouds are clearly foreign, such an exotic array
Against the blue cloth of the sky
I want to rummage among them, I want to turn them over
With eager fingers, I want to bargain
For this one and that one, I want to haggle and dicker
Over the prices, and see my clouds wrapped up
In sheets of old newspapers, and give them away
To young girls to pin in their hair
Or tuck them, glossy as gardenias, behind an ear.

A LAST SUPPER

What an incongruous party! In this Last Supper
Thirteen men, black as Ethiopians
Are crowded at a table, horseshoe shaped
And surely groaning under the weight
Of huge hands of bananas, whole fish, and watermelons
Split open to show their sweet, black-seeded flesh.
Some of the men are eating, some of them
Reach out toward the food, or toward the table;
They are all facing forward, although
There are two tiers of them, and those in the rear
Will never get anything. This one, I think,
Must be the Jesus, although he looks
Exactly like the others. He sits in the middle,
And one of his hands is raised, it might be in blessing.
After all, might the event have been more like this
Than like a Renaissance painting, crowded and Italian—
Just thirteen simple men coming together
To partake of whatever the season offers,
Not knowing which among them will be the betrayer,
None of them knowing how the story will end.

NOON

Because it is noon again
All the bells in the world are ringing;
Because these steep streets,
These walls smothered in climbing flowers

Tumbling downhill like a cataract
Have weathered another night
A cataract of sound erupts from the iron throats
Of all the bells in the world.

There is no escaping this praise,
This torrent of congratulation
On having once again survived the night-hazards,
Perilous passage where the spirit stumbles,

The insomniac tosses on a dreamless ocean,
The lonely one turns to the bottle as to a lover,
The exile dreams of a home that never was.
Because the darkness is real, the bells are ringing;

Because the sun has crawled over the hills once more
All the bells in the world are praising;
Because it is noon again
They babble with iron tongues.

INTERPRETATIONS

Sometimes the barking of dogs sounds like human speech,
Like men arguing in a foreign tongue,
And the sudden glint of sunlight on a windshield
Might be a signal flashed to a confederate;
But other times the stuttering of real gunfire
Might be taken for harmless firecracker explosions,
And the screams coming from behind the police station
For simple drunken raillery.

ROMANCE

What a romantic moon
Hangs over the ragged edge of the city
Where the sidewalks ravel out into the shadows
And in the poignant dusk
A single figure waits at the curb.

He might be about to sing a baritone *addio*
In an opera by Puccini,
Or plotting to rob a bank,
Or planning to sail tomorrow for the Americas
To seek his fortune,
If he were not already there,
If he were not an ordinary neighbor
Waiting for the late bus. He is everywhere;
Inscrutable, his face gazes out
With the false simplicity of a fairy tale
From a photograph in a stranger's album,
Or through the thick impasto of the 19th century
Framed in a provincial museum.

Lately I have begun to see
How everything partakes of romance,
Even the whey-faced women staring vacantly
From the windows of the bus,
And the little lighted shop windows,
And traffic lights winking like jewels,
Emerald, topaz, clear red,
On dark, impassive faces staring up
From the whirlwind of blowing papers
In the moon-drenched gutter.

NIGHT AIR

Can it be true that the *culebra* comes in the night
And wraps its length around your throat
Without sound, and you cannot cry out?
Can it be true that the cat, greedy for milk
On the baby's lips, will suck out its breath while it sleeps?
Can it be true that a wolf lives in the wall
Even of this city apartment? Night after night
I have heard him scratching a hole in the plaster
With greedy claws. Can it be true
That somewhere in the city a woman you never met
Models an image of wax with a pin through the heart
To give you bad dreams of the viper, the cat, and the wolf?
Does the night air that breathes in the window
Carry invisible seeds, the nightmare contagion?
Can it be true that it seeps in everywhere?

IN THE STUDIO

This room demonstrates
The solid geometry of light
Cube of brightness
Sphere of silence
Cone of solitude

The room is a paradigm
Of the hollow center of the universe
A vessel of reflections
At dusk it sinks into the shadows
Still glowing with a cold radiance

AFTER ILLNESS IN CHILDHOOD

Would you believe a horse-drawn sleigh?
Would you believe a woman and her daughter
Under fur robes, being pulled swiftly along
Over snow-covered paths, between glittering dark pines?
Does Mother dream she is fleeing, or flying, to a lover?
This is not Russia, it is Lakewood, New Jersey.
The shrill humming of the runners on packed snow,
Jingle of sleighbells, the horse's steady trot
Send such waves tingling through the frosty air
I think that music is still playing
At the far edge of the atmosphere
As once the child imagined flying
Down along snowy roads forever.

THE BIG SNOW

Such an unprecedented snowfall
Made hostages of us all; in choked driveways
Stalled cars waited patiently as horses. Only voices
And flickering images, our flat familiars,
Reached into the buried houses
Bringing rumors of the customary world.
It was like being forced to listen
To the same music, on headphones,
For forty-two days.
It was like sitting in a puptent inside
An apartment house livingroom,
Not knowing whether the mobs in the street
Are coming to kill you or save you.

OUR PASSIONS ARE NEVER ACCIDENTAL

Unlikely Nurse Banziger,
Fresh as a new-made bed,
Packaged in white synthetic, an old hand
Firm on a pulse,
Describes her former life
As an Egyptian princess
(She remembers everything).
After that she came back several times,
Snared in the cage of civilization;
Died, once, of cholera, in the Caucasus.
In her present incarnation
She recites the testimony
Of others like herself, to prophesy backwards
Like Epimenides, over unresisting patients.

III

GRANDMOTHER

I have no little brown grandmother
Part of the old earth
Common as mullein
Taking a bitter tea in tiny sips
Or mumbling over dark pots;

Wanted to learn her old ways,
How she rode the devil's sidesaddle
Between thumb and forefinger,
Brewed potions and poultices,
Told fortunes in coffee cups.

Instead, my grandmother
Returns me a pallid face
So like my own
I am at a loss,
And shrink from the ghostly glass.

DANCES FOR SMALL SPACES

1.

In September, when the maples begin
To show their true colors
I'll bless myself with blue water.
Geography has nothing to do
With where I'm going,
Drifting earthward under a cloudy parachute,
Falling like a green rain over Chattanooga.

2.

A dark woman with mad eyes
Drags her sackful of secrets
Past suburban housewives
With faces white as suet.
She has never been angry enough.

3.

Once there was a time
When everything happened
Because it was meant to happen.
Now, I would like to find wild mushrooms,
Make a garden,
And bake bread every Thursday.

4.

Living in the shadow of her mother-in-law
She sees herself as a collection of floating parts.
Today she is a hand
Cut off at the wrist.

5.

Somewhere a parrot green as verdigris
With a sulfur yellow head
And a wild red eye like a monocle
Is humming softly to himself
Atop a battered iron cage.
A child dances to his tune.

HIS GARDEN

It was his garden. Watching him out there
Week after week, how he teased it out of earth
Friable, poisoned, caked and cracked with salt;
Hunkering under the trellis heavy with roses,
How he ordered the orderly rows with stakes and string
In the rank raw odor of marigolds,
Among tangles of cosmos and zinnias,
Speechless, solitary as a tree,
How he turned his back on them all,
How it burst into bloom and blossomed in his mind.

OLD WIVES' TALES

1. The Well

It was a real well, real
As any in a fairy tale
Where a frog might sit
On its mossy lip, dreaming of princesses;
Far below the stone rim
Mantled in velvet verdigris
A single watery eye stares up,
Unwinking, hypnotic, blinkered
By a wooden lid. At its side
A mundane bucket remembers the kitchen
And the stout farmwife, hoarse as a frog,
Warning of depths unplumbed, scraping crusted pots.

2. The Hedge

Higher than my head
Thicker than my outstretched arm
—Uncle had to stand on a chair
To clip it with giant shears—
How could a prince
Ever wrench his way through it?
Ah, but close to the ground
Leafy passageways and tunnels
Have been opened by the small animals of darkness.
I myself have crept out that way, unseen
By those who don't lower their eyes
Or glance sideways
But stand at attention, looking straight ahead.

3. The Slipper

Twenty years later
How could it fit a foot
Broad, calloused, no longer accustomed
To dancing? On the dusty shelf
Rackety girls, heartless and innocent,
Find mysterious souvenirs.
A wedding dress
Evokes incredulous laughter,
And as for the dancing shoes,
Surely Mother could never
Have worn something so dainty, so fragile,
So fine.

THE MUSE IS ALWAYS
THE OTHER WOMAN

He courts her up there on the roof.
Among the chimneys and flowering vines,
In the pale, lucid air
Crowded with invisible presences
He is looking for something;
He believes that, womanlike,
She will help him find it.
He is a rational man
In search of his madness,
Although all art is an illusion
And music and dance
Do not, in fact, make the corn grow
Or assist the crops to ripen.

He cries, without her the world is meaningless
As music to the tone deaf
Or the rainbow to the color blind!
He thinks today he will build
Such a curious cage
She will creep inside of her own accord;
But she has escaped him before,
Many times, on the border
Between two lives, or in the caesura
Between reason and unreason,
And makes her way alone
Through his long dream.

MARRIAGE

Every morning in the garden
Over the coffee
They swap their dreams;
Hers of running away with the scissors-grinder
For his of a tiger
In the Chase Manhattan Bank.
Such a thin, bitter brew
Exhales aromatic breath
From the steaming coffee cups,
He offers six dark men
Rearranging the stones of the street
For the grave of the gypsy queen
In Rolla, Missouri, garnished
With plastic roses, and
She counters with a size 5 wedding dress,
A closing door, for the number eleven
And his runaway horse.
She'll barter his balding
For her growing stout.
Before the pot runs dry
He pours a second cup, not dreaming
There is a snake in the garden.

BACK FAR ENOUGH,
DOWN DEEP ENOUGH

Who she was:
   the old woman rocking, impatient for her kingdom
Whence she sprang:
   from soiled loins
How she looked:
   like a maiden in May
What she wore:
   a crown of cress and gown of gossamer
Where she lived:
   in stony streets
Did she, nevertheless, laugh and sing?
   yes
The gift she coveted:
   flowers that would not fade
Where she hunted for it:
   in the mirror's blonde reflection
What she feared to find:
   the room without echoes
Why she cried:
   so someone would hear her
Who comforted her:
   no one

THE STRENGTH OF WOMEN

You could say a flower is helpless
Rooted where she stands, mute,
No fangs or talons;
Accusing no one when she is torn up,
Not even a reproach.

And you could say
There are women like that,
Drawing life from a mysterious source,
Springing up everywhere
With no need to explain themselves.

FURNISHING THE HOUSE

Close to the beach
Where a clear wash of salt water
Translucent as sunlight
Sluiced over the patterned sand,
Tiny rose-colored crabs,
All rib and claw,
Established residence
In deserted snailshells
As we've moved in
To the hollow house.
It is a series of absences:
Such airy spaces,
One opening out of the other,
Luminous, waiting, expectant, into which
We'll crowd the substance of our lives.

EL DORADO

This morning a cloud hangs between me and the mountains,
A thin gray cloud like a curtain, the color of ashes;
Beyond it the mountains are visible, but barely,
Almost timidly raising themselves from the cloudy earth
Like animals dragging enormous limbs from their burrows.
How lightly the cloud rests on the surface of the earth,
Like a gauzy shawl flung carelessly over a shoulder.
In the middle distance, clotted with dwellings and trees
Every tiny detail is clear, as sharp and distinct
As a miniature village in a museum display;
But beyond, where the cloud scrim hangs, all is mystery.
When the curtain lifts, I wonder what will appear.
Perhaps Cibola, nestled between the ridges,
Or the city of El Dorado, the golden one,
That has never been found, though men have died pursuing
Its tantalizing image and the imagined treasure
Concealed in its streets, as it lies concealed in the mountains
Whose secrets are hidden behind the cloudy veil.

ROSES AND BRICKS

To the Spaniards, every bloom was *roses*
As they followed the long dream of treasure
Toward dissolving horizons
Of a country that had yet her maidenhead
With no words for its exuberant flowering;
Whereas in another language
The self takes many forms:
A single yellow lily
Freckled with crimson spots;
A multifoliate fern;
The angel's-trumpet
With creamy, foot-long blossoms, visited
By bees and a hummingbird;
Or it might be
This inconceivable creeper, wandering Jew,
Reaching out dusty, plum-colored fingers
To grasp at nothing,
And I understand
Why the Mexicans have a dozen words for *brick*.

AESTHETICS OF THE ASYLUM

The sober reality
Was a double line of orphans in blue smocks
Marching above the blue river
Under the smoky eye of winter.
It is possible to envy them;
The picture of which they formed a part
Was so well composed,
In shades of blue and smoke
And the dull brick red of the asylum walls;
How orderly and tranquil the effect
Of the wintry ranks of children
Under the silent sky.

THE PERMANENCE OF FORM:
DEMONSTRATIONS

—after Adelbert Ames, Jr.

When, in the Capital, strange, androgynous folk
Crouch on iron gratings
Huddled in the bureaucratic exhalations
Of an island of decreasing entropy,
And, under a killer moon
Flocks of strange birds
Land on the seacoast of Florida,
That is only to demonstrate
That men and women are like sand, absorbing
Whatever falls on them, piecing their lives together
From patches of reality.

Thus, in one corner of the tilted room
A tiny man is trying to hide himself;
He thinks he has been made small
Because he has done something shameful.
In the opposite corner
An enormous child plants gigantic sneakers
Athwart the threshold of vision, demonstrating
The domination of the unseen world,
A universe filled with the souls of objects, galaxies
That whirl about us like a cloud of gnats,
Eternal as angels dancing on a pin.

ALL AROUND US

How many pallid Christs, with painted blood
And real hair, does it take to explain
A single boy spread-eagled on the floor
Of the police station, blind, baffled eyes
Still not believing what has happened to him?
There are a thousand tragedies all around us.
There is the tragedy of the dog with three legs
And the tragedy of the old uncle lying, or dying, in bed
Who turns his head away on the comfortless pillow;
The tragedy of the young girl afraid of the life within her.
I think of the tragedy of barren women,
Of the poor, who never starve, but are always hungry;
I think of the tragedy of having visions,
And that of never having visions,
And what a miracle it is that the dog still hops to his dinner
On his three legs, and the rain comes in its season
All around us, and waters weeds and garden alike.

THE OTHER LIFE

I know in my other life I am a whale
Surfacing rarely, blunt as a club, singing
In my rusty cracked voice
Like the creaking timbers of a clipper ship
Persistent cantatas mixed with the thump and swish
Of enormous waves, the ground bass
Of the ocean; or silent
To hear the answering song of distant kin.
Profound and dark, my echoing apartments.
My element is salt, like tears.
I move in it alone, light as a shadow.
Beached, I grow monstrous, helpless, and grotesque.

THE VISITORS

When they come unannounced, as angels did once,
Shedding the darkness
Of long, unimaginable roads,
And beyond two thicknesses of glass
My upstart maple, shaking in the wind,
Taps at the pane, moaning and sighing,
What if their word for *table*
Is *table,* and still we don't understand?

In muddy boots, courteous,
Making themselves at home
On the carpet, they are larger
Than life. Upstairs
In the cold bedroom, a sad guitar insists
On the delicate, silvery hieroglyphics
Of the yarrow stalks, echoing
Their incomprehensible message.

WHAT CHARITY IS

Winter at the bird feeder
Where squirrels have taken the seeds.

Skeleton trees stretch brittle arms;
A skin of ice sheathes the pond,

And every crack where bitter air could enter
Is sealed, by conscientious burghers;

Even the chimneys are stopped up
So no warmth escapes.

Under a sky blue as skim milk
No one walks in the street

Where a private in the Salvation Army
Rattles a few cold coins.

THE HUMMINGBIRDS

I could tell you about a weed as tall as a house
With graceless dull leaves and drooping panicles
Of yellow tube-like flowers, not beautiful,
And rubbishy clusters of seed pods hanging down
When the flowers fall to the ground in curdled drifts;
It grows between us and the sky, it obstructs the view;
Soon its muscular root will shove up the stone of the paving,
And commonsense voices tell us to cut it down.
But the hummingbirds have taken it for a feeding station,
And every day over our coffee we watch them suck
The honey that succors them from the milky tubes
And whip a thousand rainbows out of the air
With the tireless beating of their invisible wings.

SUMMERTIME

If Mr. Johnson comes moonlighting after work
To clear out the briars and the mulberry tree,
And spade up the ground around the honeysuckle,
Chopping out roots as thick and long as a man's leg
And turning over leafmold and gravel into the buried topsoil,
And if the boys load up the rotted wood
Of the fascia, and the rotten posts, and the crazed
Panes of the old garage doors, and truck them to the dump,
And in the neighbor's yard squash and tomatoes ripen,
And the mockingbird, *mimos polyglottos*, sings all night long,
And the fireflies light their green lanterns, and pale
Flower faces bob and sway across the dusky garden,
Then it's summertime, with the rains
Already in the wings, waiting to begin,
And the days are closing in.

THE WORLD IS FULL OF POETS

On days like this I see that the world is full of poets,
Some are lying under a tree, others on a piazza,
Some are riding the subways or streetcars, some
Far away from home, perhaps,
Look for a letter in an empty box.
They are everywhere! No boundaries contain them!
When the laurel wreaths are distributed
They will stand in a jostling procession,
Elbowing one another.
When the medals and lovingcups are given out
The line of poets will stretch from here to Brooklyn!
On days like this all the poets of the world
Might soar to the skies, arm in arm with one another
Like glorious brothers and sisters, to astonish
The world, with a single enormous hosanna.

PITT POETRY SERIES
Ed Ochester, General Editor

Shirley Kaufman, *The Floor Keeps Turning*
Shirley Kaufman, *From One Life to Another*
Shirley Kaufman, *Gold Country*
Ted Kooser, *Sure Signs: New and Selected Poems*
Larry Levis, *Wrecking Crew*
Jim Lindsey, *In Lieu of Mecca*
Tom Lowenstein, tr., *Eskimo Poems from Canada and Greenland*
Archibald MacLeish, *The Great American Fourth of July Parade*
Peter Meinke, *The Night Train and The Golden Bird*
Peter Meinke, *Trying to Surprise God*
Judith Minty, *In the Presence of Mothers*
James Moore, *The New Body*
Carol Muske, *Camouflage*
Leonard Nathan, *Dear Blood*
Leonard Nathan, *Holding Patterns*
Kathleen Norris, *The Middle of the World*
Sharon Olds, *Satan Says*
Gregory Pape, *Border Crossings*
Thomas Rabbitt, *Exile*
James Reiss, *Express*
Ed Roberson, *Etai-Eken*
Ed Roberson, *When Thy King Is A Boy*
Eugene Ruggles, *The Lifeguard in the Snow*
Dennis Scott, *Uncle Time*
Herbert Scott, *Groceries*
Richard Shelton, *Of All the Dirty Words*
Richard Shelton, *Selected Poems, 1969-1981*
Richard Shelton, *You Can't Have Everything*
Gary Soto, *The Elements of San Joaquin*
Gary Soto, *The Tale of Sunlight*
Gary Soto, *Where Sparrows Work Hard*
David Steingass, *American Handbook*
Tomas Tranströmer, *Windows & Stones: Selected Poems*
Alberta T. Turner, *Learning to Count*
Alberta T. Turner, *Lid and Spoon*
Chase Twichell, *Northern Spy*
Constance Urdang, *Only the World*
Constance Urdang, *The Lone Woman and Others*
Cary Waterman, *The Salamander Migration and Other Poems*
Bruce Weigl, *A Romance*
David P. Young, *The Names of a Hare in English*
David P. Young, *Sweating Out the Winter*